SHATTERED

Raw and Real: Finding Faith When God Feels Absent

HEIDI REIGN TAYLOR

WORDS MATTER
P U B L I S H I N G
OUR WORDS CHANGE THE WORLD

Words Matter Publishing
P.O. Box 1190
Decatur, IL 62525
www.wordsmatterpublishing.com

ISBN 13: 978-1-962467-83-4

Library of Congress Catalog Card Number: 2025938753

Table of Contents

Introduction

This book isn't about my personal tragedies—**God's still working**.

It isn't about blame-shifting, bitterness, or resentment.

It's about Jesus.

It's about how **He pulled me from the depths of despair**, how He rescued me when I thought I was too broken to be saved.

When I wrote this book, I was in **the worst spiritual storm of my entire life**. I wasn't just at rock bottom—I was below it. I had been shattered beyond all repair, or so I thought.

I didn't want to go on anymore.
I just wanted the pain to stop.

Every time I thought, *This is it. I can't take another breath,* **Jesus came to my rescue**.

Every time I thought, *There's no one out here I can really trust,* because at that point in my life, I questioned everyone's loyalty—**Jesus showed me who truly loved me and who never did**.

Every time I felt **completely alone and isolated**, He reminded me why.

- **Sometimes, when Jesus removes people from your life, it's not rejection—it's protection.**
- **Sometimes, He has to strip everything away so you can finally see that He's been there all along.**
- **Sometimes, we can't hear His voice because we are drowning in noise, in chaos, in toxic relationships, in the weight of our own heartbreak.**

But when I **let Him in**—when I finally stopped resisting and surrendered it all to Him—**everything changed.**

I realized **He was my safe place.**
Not just my Lord and Savior.
Not just my Father.
Not just my Provider.

He was also my Friend.

"I no longer call you servants, because a servant does not know his master's business. Instead, I have called you friends."

—*John 15:15*

I've been through **trauma** that crushed me to my core. I've experienced **pain** that made me feel like I was drowning.
I've been so broken that I didn't even recognize myself anymore.

I didn't understand **why God allowed any of it.**

But I made Him a promise—

"Jesus, if You heal me... if You get me through this... I will help others heal too."

I am still healing.
I am still growing.
I am still **a work in progress**.

But I know this:

"You intended to harm me, but God intended it for good to accomplish what is now being done, the saving of many lives."

—*Genesis 50:20*

None of it was in vain.

- Every tear I cried, **He counted.**
- Every betrayal I faced, **He saw.**
- Every heartbreak I endured, **He held me through it.**

God didn't allow these things **to destroy me.**

He allowed them to strengthen me.
To give me wisdom and clarity.
To reshape and mold me into who He always meant for me to be.

And everything He has done for me—
He wants to do for you, too.

- **If you feel too broken, too lost, or too far gone— Jesus is waiting for you.**
- **If you feel like you can't take another breath— Jesus is reaching for you.**
- **If you feel like you don't matter—Jesus died to prove that you do.**

I pray that this book helps you **see Him more clearly.**
I pray that it speaks to you in **your own healing.**
I pray that by the time you reach the last page, you will know **how deeply and fiercely Jesus loves you.**

If you need prayers, **reach out to me**.

I will be praying for you. **You are not alone.**

Much love, always.

Chapter 1

Months of Work—Gone.
Just Like That.

I had been working on my book for months. Something in me had whispered to buy a flash drive, just in case something happened to my laptop. That way, I could save my work and ensure it wouldn't be lost. So I did. I bought the flash drive and backed up everything.

Tonight, I sat down to work on it again. It had been a couple of weeks since I last wrote, with Christmas, work, and sickness getting in the way. But now, sitting in my new office—just a spare bedroom, really, with a wooden desk I had found on Marketplace for five dollars—I felt a mix of excitement and nervousness. That desk meant so much to me because my beautiful niece and her new husband had helped me get it and bring it home. I was ready to dive back in, but I was also apprehensive because this book wasn't just a book. It was my calling. I was writing it for God, hoping it would help others who were struggling, too.

But when I plugged in my flash drive, it was gone.

All of it.

I searched every file. Nothing. Maybe I had saved it somewhere else? Nope. I knew, without a shadow of a doubt, that I had saved it on my flash drive. I had double-checked it. I carried that drive everywhere with me so it wouldn't get lost—or worse, in case someone broke into my house and stole it or deleted it out of spite.

I'm an overthinker. In case you couldn't tell.

And when I couldn't find it, I lost it. I was so overwhelmed with emotion that I ripped the flash drive out of my laptop and threw it across the room. I screamed at God that I was done. It felt like He was telling me my work wasn't good enough, like He had tossed it in the trash. I yelled at Him, saying I hated Him, that nothing I ever did was good enough. Nothing. Everything I poured my heart into—He always seemed to take it away.

My relationships. My writing. Even my TikToks, which I made to guide and encourage people, barely got any attention. Instead, most of the comments were from men hitting on me until I had to delete and block them. I sobbed, telling God I would never be enough.

But as you, my readers, can probably tell, this wasn't just about losing my work. It was about everything.

I think sometimes, when we break down like that, it isn't just about the one thing that pushed us over the edge. It's about everything we've been holding in— every hurt, every frustration, every betrayal. Sometimes, it takes something small, something that might not seem like a big deal to others, to finally make us snap. And when we do, all of it comes pouring out. We say things we don't mean—or maybe, in that moment, we do mean them. But once the storm settles, we look back and hardly recognize the person we were in that moment.

After my meltdown, I got quiet. And that's when I heard Him.

In the stillness, in my heart, He said, *Finally, you're getting to the heart of it.*

He reminded me that His grace was sufficient. That He forgave me the moment I cried out to Him. That He still loved me, even when I didn't get it right. He didn't expect me to be perfect. He just wanted me to trust Him—even when things didn't go as planned, even when I had to start over.

He wanted me to be real—with Him and with myself. To stop striving for perfection. To stop pretending I had everything together. Because He never called us to be perfect. None of us are, and none of us ever will be. He wants us to come to Him as we are—flawed, broken, raw. He wants us to admit when we're angry with Him, to be honest about our doubts, our pain, our struggles. Because He already knows our hearts. We're not fooling Him. We can't hide from Him.

And before anyone judges me for telling God I hated Him, let me be clear: He forgave me the moment I repented. He wiped it away like it had never been said. Do I feel bad about it? Absolutely. Even looking back, I still feel ashamed. But He knew my heart then, and He knows it now.

And He wants you to know something, too.

He wants you to be real with Him about everything— your anger, your doubts, your sins, the things you struggle to let go of. He wants you to come to Him, not when you're perfect, but when you're broken.

I'm not perfect. Not even close. And I don't pretend to be. I'm ashamed of how I acted that night, but it was real. It was how I felt in that moment, and God can work with that.

I thought about taking this part out of the chapter, but God told me to leave it. Because people need to know it's okay to come to Him as they are. He doesn't ask us to fix ourselves before we approach Him. He just asks us to come.

Too often, we wear masks. We pretend our lives are perfect. Social media only makes it worse. People post their highlight reels—the perfect family, the perfect relationship, the perfect career. But what does that do for anyone? It makes others look at their own lives and wonder, *What's wrong with me? Why is my life a mess?* It creates a cycle of comparison, making people feel even more alone. They start believing that God has abandoned them, that He's punishing them. But the truth is, no one's life is perfect. Everyone struggles. Everyone falls short. Not everyone is willing to show it.

Some people are private. They're afraid of judgment. So they keep up the facade, letting their egos grow, convinced they must maintain the illusion of perfection. But who does that help? No one.

If we aren't honest about our struggles, how can others learn from us? How can they know they aren't alone in their battles? Sometimes, I think we go through hardships not just to grow ourselves, but so we can help others climb out of their own darkness. So we can be a light.

Like I said, I'm not perfect, and I won't pretend to be. If I mess up, I'll own it and do my best to make it right. I don't always lose my cool like I did that night, but when I do, I know God is with me—even in my worst moments. I regret the things I said, but that's what grace is for. Grace humbles us. It forces us to confront the parts of ourselves we'd rather ignore. And that's where healing begins.

When God humbles us, it's not to shame us. It's to mold us. To strip away our pride, our illusions, our self-righteousness, and build something stronger in its place. It's like muscle growth—when you work out, your muscles must tear before they rebuild. It's painful, but it makes you stronger.

When God humbles us, He doesn't just fix the surface. He works from the inside out, healing the deepest wounds, making us better than we were before.

And that's what this journey is about—letting Him take our broken pieces and create something beautiful.

Chapter 2

The Devil Condemns, But God Forgives

When we mess up, the devil is the first to condemn us. He whispers lies, making us believe we are beyond redemption, filling us with shame and guilt. It feels like we are beating ourselves up, as if God is disappointed in us. But let me assure you—once you apologize to God with a sincere heart, He immediately washes that sin away, as if it never happened.

God doesn't hold onto our mistakes. He looks at our hearts. If we are truly remorseful and ask for forgiveness, He sets us free. Those chains are broken, and we are no longer bound by them. This is where humility begins. True repentance humbles us, making us desire change, helping us learn from our mistakes so we don't repeat them.

Admitting when we're wrong is difficult—it takes courage. Even admitting our sins to God can feel overwhelming, and sometimes we hide from Him because we don't feel worthy of His forgiveness. But each time we come to Him in repentance, it becomes easier. Eventually, we come to know that Jesus is our safe place.

It's okay to be vulnerable with Him. He is your Father, your Friend, the One who loves you unconditionally. None of us deserve His grace, but He gives it freely. That is why He came—to suffer and die for us, to take our punishment upon Himself so that we would not have to bear it.

Imagine a loving parent rushing to their child's side, wanting to protect them from harm. That's what Jesus did for us. He saw us being tormented and beaten down by sin and stepped in to take the punishment on our behalf. He endured the cross so we wouldn't have to endure eternal separation from Him. If that's not love, then I don't know what is.

God wants you to know that you are not alone. Maybe you have lost loved ones, maybe people have walked away from you, but Jesus has never left you. He never will. He won't force His will upon you, but if you reject Him, He will graciously step back. However, the moment you call out to Him, He will come running back to you.

***

How Do You Get Closer to God?

Do you want to hear and recognize God's voice? The key is reading the Bible.

The more you immerse yourself in Scripture, the more you attune your heart to His voice. He speaks in a still, small voice—a voice of peace, love, and truth. Anything that contradicts that is not from Him.

Reading the Bible can feel overwhelming at first. The parables and deeper meanings might not always be clear. But that's what makes it the Living Word. God speaks to each of us differently through it because He has personal messages for every one of us.

One of my favorite ways to hear from God is by asking Him a question and then randomly opening my Bible. I trust that whatever passage my eyes land on, He is speaking to me through it.

For example, one day I asked God, "Why does my dating life always seem to fail?" I flipped open my Bible and landed on **Hosea 11:2-4**:

"The more they were called, the more they went away; they kept sacrificing to the Baals and burning offerings to idols. Yet it was I who taught Ephraim to walk; I took them up by their arms, but they did not know that I healed them. I led them with cords of kindness, with the bands of love, and I became to them as one who eases the yoke on their jaws, and I bent down to them and fed them."

(Hosea 11:2-4, ESV)

What I understood from this passage was simple: *Sometimes, God leads people into our lives, but that doesn't mean they will choose to stay. He may bring two people together, but it's still up to them to handle the relationship properly. Some people aren't ready for what they prayed for, and they fumble the blessing.*

If you struggle to understand Scripture, I encourage you to look up Bible commentaries online or on YouTube. Also, pray for discernment—ask God to reveal His message to you. It's helpful to read entire chapters instead of isolated verses so you can grasp the full meaning of what God is saying.

***

God Wants a Relationship, Not Religion

God doesn't want you to follow Him just because of a list of rules. He wants a personal relationship with you. Religion focuses on laws and rituals, but a relationship with God starts with love, trust, and faith.

Think about human relationships. When you love someone, you don't set a bunch of strict rules for them to follow right away. You grow together, you learn each other's hearts, and over time, you naturally begin to respect and honor each other.

That's how it is with God. He doesn't demand immediate perfection. The more you experience His love, the more you desire to live in a way that pleases Him. You'll naturally let go of the things that don't align with His peace because you won't want to disappoint Him—just like you wouldn't want to hurt someone you deeply love.

That is God working in your heart.

***

Faith: Believing in the Unseen

Many people struggle with faith because they want physical proof of God's existence. But that's what faith is—it's believing in what you cannot see.

As **Hebrews 11:1** says:

> *"Now faith is the assurance of things hoped for, the conviction of things not seen."*
>
> *(Hebrews 11:1, ESV)*

We live in a world where people demand evidence, but some things can only be understood through faith. I ask you this: *Are you willing to take the risk of rejecting God and spending eternity without Him?*

Hell is real. It is the absence of love, light, healing, and hope. It is eternal separation from God. That is not a chance I'm willing to take.

I encourage you to research personal testimonies of people who have encountered Jesus. Many who doubted Him at first became believers after experiencing Him personally. Once they encountered His love, they never turned away.

As Jesus said in **Matthew 7:7-8**:

"Ask, and it will be given to you; seek, and you will find; knock, and the door will be opened to you. For everyone who asks receives; the one who seeks finds; and to the one who knocks, the door will be opened."

(Matthew 7:7-8, NIV)

So seek Him. Ask Him to reveal Himself to you in a way that is personal and undeniable.

If you are searching for faith, tell God what you need in order to believe. He will meet you where you are and show you He's real.

***

God Is Waiting for You

God loves you unconditionally. He isn't waiting for you to be perfect before coming to Him—He wants you just as you are, flaws and all. He wants honesty, not perfection.

You don't have to earn His love. It's already yours.

So come to Him, seek Him, and trust Him. He will never leave you, and He will never forsake you.

Chapter 3

Letting Go

This is a hard one. Letting go of the people I love most has been one of the hardest things I've ever had to do. And it doesn't matter in what form it happens—whether through death, breakups, or people walking out on me, the pain is still there.

I blame it all on the devil.

He comes to **steal, kill, and destroy**.

As John 10:10 says:

> "The thief comes only to steal and kill and destroy. I came that they may have life and have it abundantly. I am the good shepherd. The good shepherd lays down his life for the sheep."

> *(John 10:10, ESV)*

The devil is sneaky. He is a coward, and what do cowards do? They **hide and lie**. They manipulate, deceive, and plant seeds of fear and doubt because they are afraid of the truth. But **God says the truth will set us free**.

> *"So Jesus said to the Jews who had believed him, 'If you abide in my word, you are truly my disciples, and you will know the truth, and the truth will set you free.'"*
>
> *(John 8:31-32, ESV)*

What I've learned about letting go is this: **God was protecting me**.

He was protecting me from something that was already hurting me or something that would have hurt me even more in the future. He was drawing me closer to Him in those moments of separation, using that time to reshape me, to mold me into the person He always meant for me to be.

I've always known the person I am today was deep inside of me, but I never imagined the **hell** I would have to endure for her to emerge.

And yet, despite the pain, I wouldn't change a thing.

Because **who I am now**—closer to Jesus, stronger in faith, and free from what once held me back—is worth every bit of suffering. **He is my safe place.** And before Him, I never truly had a safe place.

***

When God Asks You to Let Go

When God asks you to let something—or someone—go, it is **not** to hurt you. Yes, the pain may feel unbearable, but pain also **shapes us**. It strengthens us. It keeps us from running back to what once broke us.

If God is asking you to give someone up, it's because **He knows** that deep down, they were already hurting you in some way. Maybe not in ways you could see, but **God sees everything**. He hears conversations we don't. He knows people's hearts in ways we never will.

But what about when He takes away **good people**? What about when we lose loved ones to death? That is a much harder question to answer.

Losing a parent, a spouse, a child, a sibling, or a dear friend can make us question everything. But even in those moments, **God promises to be with us**.

"Good people pass away; the godly often die before their time. But no one seems to care or wonder why. No one seems to understand that God is protecting them from the evil to come. For those who follow godly paths will rest in peace when they die."

(Isaiah 57:1-2, NLT)

I know this doesn't make the loss easier. But **God knows things we don't.** He sees what's ahead, and sometimes, taking someone home is His way of protecting them from something far worse.

Bad things happen because **this world belongs to the devil**.

Revelation 12:7-12 tells us that after Satan was cast out of Heaven, he was thrown **down to Earth**:

"Woe to you, O earth and sea, for the devil has come down to you in great wrath, because he knows that his time is short!"

(Revelation 12:7-12, ESV)

***

What About Those Who Didn't Follow God?

This is a question that used to **terrify** me.

I have lost people who didn't seem to follow God, and the thought of them being in **Hell** was unbearable. It made me question my faith. It made me afraid to trust God.

Then, a friend of mine—Callie, my sister in Christ—shared something with me that gave me hope. She reminded me of **the thief on the cross**.

> *"One of the criminals who were hanged railed at him, saying, 'Are you not the Christ? Save yourself and us!' But the other rebuked him, saying, 'Do you not fear God, since you are under the same sentence of condemnation? And we indeed justly, for we are receiving the due reward of our deeds; but this man has done nothing wrong.' And he said, 'Jesus, remember me when you come into your kingdom.' And he said to him, 'Truly, I say to you, today you will be with me in paradise.'"*
>
> *(Luke 23:39-43, ESV)*

Even in **his final moments**, that thief **turned to Jesus** and was saved.

I believe that **before someone takes their last breath, Jesus comes to them one last time**. He gives them one final choice. He offers them **one last chance** to follow Him into eternity.

I hold onto that belief with all my heart.

***

The Danger of Idolizing People

There's another reason why **letting go** is so important: **God wants us to love Him first.**

It's easy to put people on pedestals. We pour every-thing into them, and when they leave—whether by choice or by force—it feels like our entire world is crashing down.

This is why we **must keep our focus on God**.

If we love Him first, then no matter what happens—no matter who walks away or who betrays us—we will **still stand**.

People will fail us. **God never will.**

***

A Message for Those in Pain

If you're reading this and feel like you've lost every-thing, if you feel like you **can't go on**, please hear me:

The devil is lying to you.

He wants you to believe there's nothing left to live for. That no one cares. That the world would be better off without you.

Don't listen to him.

Run to God. Pour your pain into Him. Let Him heal you.

If you're struggling with thoughts of giving up, remem-ber this: **If you are not here to pray for the people you love, who will?**

There is so much happening in the **spiritual realm** that we cannot see. God is working in ways beyond our understanding.

So don't give up.

Keep fighting. Keep believing. Keep trusting.

Because **you've got this.**

Because God's got you.

Chapter 4

Owning It

Own it. All of it.

The trauma. The pain. The dysfunction.

I once saw a post on Facebook that said:

> *"It's often the changes we didn't plan for that change us the most."*
>
> *—Girl Hush and Pray*

That quote made me reflect on the hardest part of my journey—the realization that we have to **own what happened**, even if we never intended to cause pain or even if we didn't fully understand what was happening at the time.

We must take responsibility.

We must **own our part**—the wounds we caused, the dysfunction we contributed to, the choices we made that led to pain. Even if we didn't know better, even if we never meant to hurt anyone, we still have to acknowledge it.

There's a quote by Louis C.K. that says:

> *"If someone tells us we hurt them, we don't get to decide that we didn't."*

It's a hard pill to swallow, but **we mess up.** We make mistakes. We have to own them, apologize sincerely, and do our best to make things right.

Then comes the hardest part—**learning to forgive ourselves for what we didn't know**.

Because if we don't, that guilt and regret will **eat us alive**.

***

Parenting Without Instructions

They say kids don't come with instructions, but the truth is, **they do.**

There are books, guides, and even scriptures that give us direction. But when we're in the middle of raising them, we don't always see it that way. We assume that **loving them is enough**—that if we do our best, if we apologize when we mess up, if we show them kindness and patience, it will all work out.

But sometimes, **our best isn't enough**.

Sometimes, we don't realize the impact of our actions— or our inactions—until it's **too late**.

And when hidden truths come out, when traumas are revealed that we didn't even know existed, it's like a **gut punch**. We look back and dissect every moment, searching for where it all went wrong.

But when it reaches that point, **remorse and apologies may not be enough** for an unhealed child—even if that child is now an adult. **They are still in pain.**

And **we have to accept that.**

***

31

Releasing Them to God

If your child—your grown son or daughter—comes to you with their pain, even in anger, **listen**. Even if their words cut deep, **don't take offense**.

They are speaking from years of bottled-up hurt. **This is their healing journey.** And our role in that moment is to:

- Acknowledge their pain.
- Apologize sincerely.
- Ask for their forgiveness.
- **Trust God to do the rest.**

Because **God is the only one who can truly heal them.**

And sometimes, that healing may require **distance**.

They may cut you out of their lives. They may keep your grandchildren from you. And as a parent, that is **a pain like no other**. But as much as it hurts, sometimes **we have to let them go** so they can heal—**with or without us**.

That is what unconditional love looks like.

And if they ever come back, if they ever decide to talk or go to counseling, let them know you support that. But in the meantime, **pray for them.** Pray that God will fix what has been broken.

And above all, **forgive yourself.**

***

The Prodigal Child

Karen Wheaton, a powerful woman of faith I listen to on YouTube, once spoke about **Prodigal Children**. She said:

> *"It's like heart surgery. Your Prodigal Child is on the operating table, and God is the surgeon. While He is working on them, you are in the waiting room."*

You can't have access to them right now.

But **God does.**

And He is working on them in ways you can't see. **Trust Him.**

If you've never listened to Karen Wheaton before, I encourage you to. She is a Pentecostal preacher and gospel singer, and though I'm not Pentecostal, her words **come from God**. She has lived through this exact battle, and **God brought her child home.**

If He did it for her, **He can do it for you too.**

***

Holding Onto Hope

I have seen parents take their own lives because they couldn't bear the pain of being cut off by their children. But I'm here to tell you:

Do not lose hope.

Do not make a **permanent decision** based on something that might be **temporary**.

If God has given you a vision, a dream of healing and reunion, then **hold onto that promise**.

If you need to **scream, cry, and pour your heart out to God**, then do it. Be raw. Be real. **He can handle it.**

And He has a promise for you:

"Keep your voice from weeping, and your eyes from tears, for there is a reward for your work, declares the Lord, and they shall come back from the land of the enemy. There is hope for your future, declares the Lord, and your children shall come back to their own country."

(Jeremiah 31:15-17, ESV)

"When the time is right, I, the Lord, will make it happen."

(Isaiah 60:22, ESV)

"Instead of your shame, there shall be a double portion... Therefore, in their land, they shall possess a double portion; they shall have everlasting joy."

(Isaiah 61:7, ESV)

Write these scriptures down. Tape them on your walls. Read them out loud.

Because **you are in a spiritual battle**.

And the devil **loses every time** when you stand firm in faith.

***

Spiritual Battles Require Spiritual Vision

When we face family struggles, we must **see them for what they really are—spiritual battles**.

The devil **comes to kill, steal, and destroy**. He will use the people you love the most to break you. But remember:

They are not the enemy.

The devil is.

> *"The thief comes only to steal and kill and destroy. I came that they may have life and have it abundantly."*
>
> *(John 10:10, ESV)*

God sees **everything**—every betrayal, every heartbreak, every tear. And though we don't always understand His ways, **He promises to work all things for good.**

***

Forgive Yourself

Before you come down on yourself—or judge someone else—remember this:

God looks at the heart more than the sin.

If He sees that you are truly sorry...

If He sees that you have tried to make things right...

If He sees that you have repented and owned up to your mistakes...

Then **who are you to refuse to forgive yourself?**

Jesus already paid the price.

You are not your past.
You are not your mistakes.
You are not your circumstances.

So say it out loud:
"I forgive myself for what I didn't know."
"I forgive myself for my mistakes."
"God forgives me, and I receive His grace."

Keep working on you. Keep trusting God. Keep believing for restoration.

Because you've got this.

Because God's got you.

And **God's got your babies.**

Chapter 5

Stress and Anxiety

Last night, I was trying to work on something, but I was so overwhelmed with **stress and anxiety** that I couldn't think, move forward, or do anything at all. It felt like I was **paralyzed with fear**.

Then, in my heart, I heard **Jesus speak to me**.

"Go get some rest, and we will work on it together in the morning."

So that's what I did.

I only slept three hours, but it was a **peaceful three hours**. And if I need a nap later, I'll take one.

***

Even Jesus Felt Anxiety

Do you know who else felt deep anxiety and fear? **Jesus did.**

The night before His execution, He was so overwhelmed that He begged God to **let the cup pass from Him**. He was in such agony that **He cried tears of blood**.

> Then he said to them, "My soul is very sorrowful, even to death; remain here, and watch with me." And going a little farther, he fell on his face and prayed, saying, "My Father, if it be possible, let this cup pass from me; nevertheless, not as I will, but as you will." And he came to the disciples and found them sleeping. And he said to Peter, "So, could you not watch with me one hour? Watch and pray that you may not enter into temptation. The spirit indeed is willing, but the flesh is weak."
>
> (Matthew 26:38-41, ESV)

Jesus experienced **the most intense stress imaginable**. The anxiety was so extreme that He suffered from **hematohidrosis**, a rare condition where the capillary blood vessels that feed the sweat glands rupture, causing blood to mix with sweat. It happens when a person is under **extreme physical or emotional distress**.

That's how **real** His suffering was.

But despite His fear, **He still chose to follow God's will**.

***

Fear and Anxiety Do Not Come from God

It has been my experience that when I am in a state of **fear, panic, or anxiety**, my **emotions take over**.

And when emotions take the lead, we:

- Stop thinking clearly.
- Become overwhelmed.
- React in haste.
- Hide from challenges instead of facing them.

When we allow fear and anxiety to take control, we forget that **these emotions do not come from God**.

So, how did **Jesus** handle His own fear?

He went to **God in prayer**.

He poured out His heart and **surrendered everything** to His Father.

"My Father, if it be possible, let this cup pass from me; nevertheless, not as I will, but as you will."

That moment right there? That's **faith in action**.

Even while facing death, Jesus still trusted God's greater plan. He knew that what He was about to endure would **save us all from Hell**. He **chose us** over His own comfort, His own fear, His own pain.

That is love.

***

Jesus Would Have Done It Just for You

Do you know that if **you were the only person on earth**, Jesus still would have chosen to suffer and die for you?

That's how much He loves you.

It wasn't just about saving the world. **It was personal.** It was about saving **you**.

Because He doesn't want anyone to be lost.

"It is not the will of my Father who is in heaven that one of these little ones should perish."

(Matthew 18:14, ESV)

Jesus came to save **everyone**. But not everyone will accept Him.

***

The Choice to Follow Jesus

One of the hardest things to understand is **why some people reject Jesus**.

People mock Him.
People deny Him.
People blame Him for the world's suffering.

Yet, these same people get **angry at God** when they hear that **not everyone will go to Heaven**.

But think about it—why would someone **want** to spend eternity with someone they hate?

That would be like moving into the house of a person you despise. Imagine **choosing** to live with someone who you don't believe in, don't respect, and don't love.

It would be **miserable**.

Jesus doesn't force Himself on anyone. He doesn't **insist** that we follow Him.

Instead, **He gives us a choice**.

"Many are called, but few are chosen."

(Matthew 22:14, ESV)

What does that mean?

It means **everyone is called**—everyone has been **invited**. But **only a few respond**.

Because **choosing Jesus is exactly that—a choice**.

Jesus already chose **you**. No matter what you've done, no matter where you've been, **He still chooses you**. But **He won't force you to choose Him back**.

That's what **true love** looks like.

***

Love Means Letting Go

Jesus is not pushy.

He won't chase you down.
He won't manipulate you.
He won't force His way into your life.

He simply **loves you**.

And **real love** isn't controlling.

Real love says:

> *"I love you, and I want to be with you, but I will let you decide for yourself."*

That is what Jesus does.

He loves you so much that He is willing to **let you go** if you don't want Him.

But that love is still there. Always.

And He is waiting, with open arms, **for the day you choose to come home to Him**.

***

Putting it Altogether

Stress and anxiety are **real battles**. But when fear tries to take over, **follow Jesus' example**.

- **Go to God in prayer.**
- **Be honest about your struggles.**
- **Surrender it all to Him.**

Jesus understands **exactly** how you feel.

And no matter what, **He will always choose you**.

The only question is—**will you choose Him?**

Chapter 6

Dream—Meeting Jesus at the Gazebo

Choosing Jesus is **not** like an arranged marriage.

If you don't want to be there, He will **respect your choice**. But if you ever change your mind, He will still be there—**waiting for you with open arms**.

I once had a dream that I will never forget.

It was **nighttime**, and I was walking through a **vast, open field**. On either side of me were two **tall, strong men**, each carrying a **silver sword**. They wore **armor**, and though no one spoke, I **felt protected**.

We walked in silence until we arrived at a **gazebo**.

And there—**waiting for me**—was **Jesus**.

The two men **left without a word**, and I knew they had simply brought me to Him.

During this time in my life, I was struggling with a deep conflict in my heart. A loved one had **turned away from Jesus**, and I couldn't imagine **being in Heaven without him**.

No matter what anyone told me—no matter how much they tried to convince me otherwise—I refused to accept the idea of eternity **without my loved one**.

But did I really understand what I was saying?

Did I truly grasp the **weight** of that decision?

Because **choosing to be without my loved one also meant choosing to be without Jesus.**

***

The Meeting with Jesus

I sat down on the ledge of the gazebo while Jesus stood, looking out through an **open window-like space**.

He lifted His arm and made a **gentle sweeping motion**, as if to show me **the whole world**—the **darkness**, the **stars**, the **endless trees stretching into the night**.

Though I can't remember His exact words, I **listened closely**. It felt like we were there for **an entire hour**.

And when He finished speaking, **I didn't want to leave**.

But Jesus walked me to the **center of the gazebo**, where the two men—who I now realized were **angels**— were waiting for me.

Then, Jesus turned to me, and He **hugged me**.

It was the most **gentle, loving embrace**—but it **felt like goodbye**.

I could feel it in His presence... **He loved me, but He was letting me go**.

Not because He wanted to. Not because He didn't care.

But because I **was the one choosing to walk away**.

I woke up feeling **heartbroken**.

I didn't want to be separated from Him. I didn't want to be **without Jesus**.

But I still **couldn't let go** of my loved one.

And I didn't realize it at the time, but this dream was a **warning**.

It wasn't Jesus **rejecting me**—it was Him **respecting my decision**.

***

Dream 2: Getting Thrown Out of the Church

Some time later, I had **another dream**.

I was sitting **alone in the front pew** of a church, waiting for the speaker to arrive.

I turned to look behind me and saw my **loved ones sitting in the very back**.

Even though we weren't sitting together, I felt **at peace**. Just knowing they were **in the church with me** was enough.

A **man walked in**—older, wise-looking—**the speaker**.

He held an **open Bible** with **notes** tucked inside.

I thought he was going to **preach**, but he didn't.

Instead, he looked at us **with sadness**, pointed toward the door, and without saying much, he **sent us away— out into the dark hallway**.

***

Walking in Darkness

We all got up and **left together**, walking side by side down **a long, dark hallway**.

For a brief moment, I felt **happy** just to be **with my loved ones**.

But something was wrong.

I **felt their hatred toward me**.

Even though we were together, I could **feel their resentment**—the bitterness, the anger, the **pure hatred** they had for me.

And suddenly, I realized something **horrifying**...

I **didn't feel Jesus.**

Not only did my loved ones **despise me**, but **Jesus was gone**.

I was in Hell.

The absence of love, the emptiness, the coldness of **that place**—it was **all-consuming**.

I could feel **hopelessness** in its purest form.

No love.
No kindness.
No compassion.
No joy.
No hope.

It was **all gone**.

Because **Jesus let us go**.

***

Without Jesus, There Is Nothing

That dream shook me **to my core**.

Because in that moment, I **understood the truth**—without **Jesus**, we have **nothing**.

Jesus **is love**.
Jesus **is hope**.

Jesus **is light**.
Jesus **is kindness**.

And if you remove **all those things**—if you take away **every ounce of love, peace, joy, and compassion**—what you have left is **Hell**.

***

Letting Go and Trusting God

One thing I've learned is that **if we love others more than Jesus, He will remove them.**

Sometimes, if someone is **not good for us**, God will **allow them to hurt us** so that we are **forced to let them go**.

Because if we **refuse** to set boundaries…
If we **excuse** their behavior…
If we **enable** their mistreatment of us…

We are blocking what God is trying to do in their lives.

Sometimes, **we are in God's way**.

And He needs us to **step aside** so He can do His work.

***

Codependency and Letting God Be God

I used to believe that if people **needed me**, they wouldn't leave me.

I thought that if I provided everything they needed, they would **love me back**.

But that's not **love**—that's **codependency**.

And the truth is, **they don't need me**.

They need Jesus.

And so do I.

***

A Simple Takeaway

God does **not** want anyone to perish.

He doesn't want anyone to suffer or be in pain.

He loves **you**.
He loves **them**.
He wants to **heal** all of you.

So **trust Him**.

- **Pray for discernment.**
- **Ask for wisdom.**
- **Surrender those you love to Him.**

And if they are mistreating you, **let them go**.

Not because you don't love them, but because **you do**.

You are not rejecting them—you are **entrusting them to Jesus**.

Because only **He** can save them.

***

You Are the Generational Curse Breaker

This is **not an easy walk**.

It will be **painful**.
It will be **lonely**.
It will be **hard**.

But staying in toxic relationships? **That's painful too.**

The difference is this: **one path leads to healing. The other doesn't.**

So choose healing.

Choose Jesus.

You are the **generational curse breaker**.

And you **can** do this.

But only **through Him.**

Because Jesus is the only way.

Chapter 7

Heart Surgery and the Great Physician

God will guide you through **every storm** you face.

Remember—He has **already gone before you**.

He has prepared the way, lined up the right people, and placed teachers along your journey—people who will help guide you **through the trials ahead**.

***

Seeing the Devil's Schemes

At the beginning of **one of the worst trials of my life**, I could **see the devil's schemes**.

I saw how he was working **in secret**, trying to **destroy my life** and the relationships I cherished the most.

When I recognized it for what it was, I turned to a **trusted friend, Diana**—a woman of faith who loves God with all her heart.

She **prayed for me** and directed me to **Karen Wheaton** on YouTube. (I mentioned her in an earlier chapter.)

Karen Wheaton once had a **prodigal daughter**, and she speaks from experience—encouraging those of us who are waiting for our **prodigals to return**.

She explains that when our **loved ones cut us out of their lives**, when they are not in a place to hear us, it is because **they are in heart surgery**.

And **God is their surgeon**.

We are in the waiting room.

And sometimes, **the wait is long**.

But while we wait, we must:

- **Keep praying.**
- **Keep believing.**
- **Keep speaking the Word of God over them.**

Because this is **not** just a personal struggle—**this is a spiritual battle.**

And the devil is after **our loved ones**.

Whether it's a **prodigal child, a prodigal spouse, or a prodigal friend**—the enemy wants to steal, kill, and destroy. But **God is fighting for them.**

***

The Molding Process

Sometimes, God will **remove everyone from your life** so that the **only One you have left is Him**.

And that can feel **lonely.**

But it is part of **the molding process**.

Healing and growth **are painful**—no matter if it's physical, emotional, or spiritual. Healing **hurts**.

I tell my patients this all the time:

Healing is hard, but it's worth it.

And as you heal in the places where you were broken, you **become stronger**. You won't go back to the things that **broke you** in the first place because you won't want to experience **that pain again**.

- You will learn **discernment**.
- You will learn **how to hear God's voice**.
- You will learn **to trust Him completely**.
- You will experience **a peace beyond understanding**.

"And the peace of God, which transcends all understanding, will guard your hearts and your minds in Christ Jesus."

(Philippians 4:7, NIV)

And when you are faced with challenges, you will remember:

"I can do all this through Him who gives me strength."

(Philippians 4:13, NIV)

***

God's Jealous Love

God wants to be **the most important one in your life**.

He is a **jealous God**—but **not in the way we experience jealousy as humans**.

His jealousy is not rooted in insecurity. **It is rooted in love.**

Imagine suffering **for someone you love**—giving everything, even your life—only for them to **turn away from you** and choose something that will **ultimately destroy them**.

That is what we do to God when we **choose the world over Him**.

And because He loves us, He will **correct us**.

Not out of anger. Not out of hatred.

But out of love.

***

God's Discipline Is Love

Just like a loving parent **disciplines their child**, God corrects those He loves.

> *"For the Lord disciplines the one He loves and chastises every son whom He receives."*
>
> *(Hebrews 12:6, ESV)*

A good parent doesn't discipline their child **out of cruelty**. They do it because they want to **teach them right from wrong**.

God is the same way.

> *"For the moment, all discipline seems painful rather than pleasant, but later it yields the peaceful fruit of righteousness to those who have been trained by it."*
>
> *(Hebrews 12:11, ESV)*

God doesn't correct you **to harm you**—He corrects you **to make you better**.

Because He **loves you too much** to let you **stay the same**.

***

Enduring Hardship with Faith

God's correction is meant to **humble us**.

It is in our **hardest moments** that we are most likely to **turn to Him**.

That's why **we cannot deny anyone their hardships—** because **it is in those places that they come to God**.

> *"If we endure hardship, we will reign with Him. If we deny Him, He will deny us."*
>
> *(2 Timothy 2:12, ESV)*

That's why **we must endure**.

> *"Blessed is the one who perseveres under trial because, having stood the test, that person will receive the crown of life that the Lord has promised to those who love Him."*

> *(James 1:12, NIV)*

So **don't give up**.

Even when it's hard.

Even when it feels hopeless.

Because God has **already worked everything out for your good.**

> *"And we know that in all things God works for the good of those who love Him, who have been called according to His purpose."*

> *(Romans 8:28, NIV)*

***

Answering the Call

God has called **everyone**.

But **not everyone answers**.

He is calling **you**.

Will you answer?

Because I promise you this: **you will not be disappointed if you do.**

If you feel like you've **lost everything**...

If you feel like you have **nothing left to live for**...

If you feel like **all hope is gone**...

Then **hang on**.

Hold onto the **hem of Jesus' garment**.

Cry out **His name**.

Because when you do, **He will come running to you.**

Chapter 8

The Spiritual Battle

We are all in the midst of **a spiritual battle**.

It feels like we're **being attacked from all sides**.

Everywhere we turn—at home, at work, on social media, in public, even in traffic—there's another **struggle, another fight, another battle**.

It's exhausting. It's **relentless**.

But we must remember **who the real enemy is**.

> *"For we do not wrestle against flesh and blood, but against the rulers, against the authorities, against the cosmic powers over this present darkness, against the spiritual forces of evil in the heavenly places."*
>
> *(Ephesians 6:12, ESV)*

The **real battle** isn't with people.

Not with your co-worker.
Not with your family.
Not with the person attacking you online.

It is a **spiritual battle**, and the devil is behind it—**pulling strings, stirring up division, planting seeds of anger, resentment, and confusion.**

***

The Armor of God

So how do we fight back?

God has given us the **armor we need** to stand firm against the enemy's attacks.

> *"Put on the whole armor of God, that you may be able to stand against the schemes of the devil."*
>
> *(Ephesians 6:11, ESV)*

1. **The Belt of Truth** – Stay grounded in God's truth.
2. **The Breastplate of Righteousness** – Live in righteousness and integrity.

3. **The Gospel of Peace** – Walk in peace, even in chaos.
4. **The Shield of Faith** – Trust God to protect you from the enemy's fiery darts.
5. **The Helmet of Salvation** – Guard your mind and thoughts with the assurance of your salvation.
6. **The Sword of the Spirit** – Use **God's Word** as your weapon against the enemy.

"Praying at all times in the Spirit, with all prayer and supplication."

(Ephesians 6:18, ESV)

Prayer is **not** just part of the battle—**prayer is the battle**.

When we **get on our knees and pray**, the devil **loses every time**.

***

When Breakthrough Feels Delayed

Have you been **praying for a breakthrough** and still haven't seen it?

Don't be discouraged.

Sometimes breakthroughs **take longer** because other hearts are involved.

Sometimes the only thing **left for us to do** is to **pray and trust God**.

This is where faith comes in.

When we don't see results with our **physical eyes**, we must shift our focus to our **spiritual eyes**.

God is still working.

Even when we don't see it.

Even when it feels like nothing is happening.

The moment you start praying, **the war begins in the spiritual realm**.

You are standing in the gap, **interceding** for your loved ones, **pulling them away from the enemy**.

You may not see the battle, but **it is happening**.

***

The Esther Fast: A Weapon in Spiritual Warfare

There is a fast known as the **Esther Dry Fast**—a **three-day fast** where you eat and drink **nothing**.

Before considering this fast, it is **critical** to:

- **Pray for confirmation.** Ask God if this is the fast He wants you to do.
- **Check with your doctor.** If you have health conditions or take medications, seek medical advice first.
- **Prepare yourself physically and mentally.** This is not a fast to enter into lightly.

I am about to start this **three-day fast** myself.

I won't lie—I'm **nervous** about what it will do to my body.

But this is **not about me**.

This is about **a loved one**.

This is about **a battle only God can win**.

And so, like Jesus in the wilderness, I am **choosing to trust God completely**.

"Then Jesus was led up by the Spirit into the wilderness to be tempted by the devil. And after fasting forty days and forty nights, he was hungry."

(Matthew 4:1-2, ESV)

Jesus was hungry.

Jesus was tired.

Jesus was tempted.

But He **kept His focus** on the reason for His suffering.

And He **rebuked the devil**.

"Be gone, Satan! For it is written, 'You shall worship the Lord your God, and Him only shall you serve.'"

(Matthew 4:10, ESV)

When you **resist the devil**, he **flees**.

***

Fasting in Secret

The Bible tells us that when we fast, we should **not** announce it to others.

"And when you fast, do not look gloomy like the hyp-ocrites, for they disfigure their faces that their fasting may be seen by others. Truly, I say to you, they have received their reward."

(Matthew 6:16, ESV)

That's why I haven't told anyone about my fast.

By the time this book is published and you are reading this, the fast will already be **over**.

And so will the **breakthrough I'm praying for**.

I say that in **faith**—because in God's eyes, it is **already done**.

***

The War Has Already Been Won

This morning, when I opened my **ESV Study Bible**, it landed on **the theme of Revelation**.

And I knew—**this was God's reminder** of why we fight this battle.

"Revelation unveils the unseen spiritual war in which the church is engaged: the cosmic conflict between God and His Christ on one hand and Satan and his evil allies (both demonic and human) on the other. In this conflict, Jesus the Lamb has already won the decisive victory through His sacrificial death."

(ESV Study Bible, Introduction to Revelation)

The war has already been won.

Jesus **has already conquered the enemy**.

Our job now is to **stand firm**.

To **trust Him**.

To **fight the good fight of faith**.

***

When You Haven't Seen Your Breakthrough Yet

If you are still **waiting for your breakthrough**, don't give up.

There was once a father who prayed for his **adult son** to turn back to Jesus.

But the son's heart was hardened.

The father developed **cancer** and was **dying**.

Someone asked him, *"When you get to Heaven, what will you say to God?"*

He answered, *"I will ask about my son."*

Shortly after, **the father died**.

And **after his death**, the son finally **gave his life to Christ**.

The father didn't get to see it **on earth**.

But Jesus told him **the moment he got to Heaven**.

So if you are **still waiting**...

Keep praying.
Keep believing.
Keep standing firm.

Because **God is still working.**

Even when you don't see it.

Even if you don't witness it **on this side of eternity**.

Your prayers are moving mountains.

***

You Are an Intercessor

Your **role** in this battle is **to intercede**.

To stand in the gap.

To step between your loved ones and **the devil himself** and declare:

"No, Satan! You cannot have them!"

So don't stop fighting.

Don't stop praying.

And most of all—**don't check out early**.

Your loved ones **need you**.

You've got this.

Because of the **One who's got you.**

And He never loses.

Chapter 9

Who's Your Judas?

Do you know who **Judas** was?

He was **one of Jesus' twelve apostles**—one of the closest people to Him.

And yet, **he betrayed Jesus**.

In the **Garden of Gethsemane**, Judas identified Jesus to the **Sanhedrin** by greeting Him with a **kiss**—a symbol of **love and loyalty twisted into an act of betrayal**.

"Then one of the Twelve, the one called Judas Iscariot, went to the chief priests and asked, 'What are you willing to give me if I deliver him over to you?' So they counted out for him thirty pieces of silver. From

then on Judas watched for an opportunity to hand him over."

(Matthew 26:14-16, NIV)

And afterward, **Judas regretted it**.

He was **so overcome with guilt** that he took his own life.

"So Judas threw the money into the temple and left. Then he went away and hanged himself."

(Matthew 27:5, NIV)

But **he didn't have to die like that**.

If **Judas had gone back to Jesus,** if he had **repented** and asked for forgiveness, **Jesus would have forgiven him**.

Judas didn't have to carry that weight alone. **Neither do you**.

Nothing you have done and nothing that has been done to you is worth taking your life over.

***

Recognizing Your Judas

Have you been **betrayed by someone you love deeply**?

That one person who:

- **Knows you better than anyone else**.
- **You love unconditionally**.
- **You never imagined would hurt you**.

That person might be **your Judas**.

And because of your deep love for them, their betrayal **cuts deeper than any other wound**.

But here's the truth: **this is a spiritual battle.**

It is **not** just about them.

It is **not** just about you.

There is a **bigger fight** happening behind the scenes.

***

How to Heal From Betrayal

1. Lean on Jesus

Jesus understands **exactly** how you feel.

He knows what it's like to be betrayed by someone **He loved**.

And because He endured it, **He will walk with you through it.**

2. Forgive Your Judas

This is the hardest part.

But **forgiveness is not for them**—it is for **you**.

> *"But if you do not forgive others their sins, your Father will not forgive your sins."*
>
> *(Matthew 6:15, NIV)*

Forgiveness **does not mean** excusing their behavior.

It does not mean **letting them back into your life**.

It means **releasing the burden of resentment** so that **it no longer controls you**.

3. Pray for Your Judas

I know this seems impossible.

How do you pray for someone who has **broken you**?

But your Judas needs your prayers **more than ever**.

Because **one day**, they will come face-to-face with what they have done.

And you don't want them to take **the same path Judas took**.

***

Setting Boundaries and Walking Away

Let me be clear:

Forgiving **does not** mean staying.

You do **not** have to keep **letting them hurt you**.

If someone is harming you **physically, emotionally, or mentally**, it is **not your job to save them**.

It is your job to **remove yourself** from the situation and **give them over to Jesus**.

Picture this in your mind:

You are physically **handing them over** to Jesus—placing them **into His hands** and stepping aside.

You are **not abandoning them**.

You are **trusting God to do what you cannot**.

And **yes, you may feel guilty at first**.

But **letting go with love is not the same as giving up on them**.

It is **releasing them into God's care**—where they belong.

***

Reflecting on Your Role in the Betrayal

It is also important to ask yourself:

- **What choices did I make that kept me in this situation for so long?**

- **Did I ignore red flags?**
- **Did I allow repeated disrespect?**
- **Did I make excuses for their behavior?**
- **Have I struggled with self-worth and confidence?**

This is **not** about victim-blaming.

It is about **understanding why we allow certain behaviors**—so that **we don't allow them again**.

When we know our **true identity in Christ**, we are **not afraid to set boundaries**.

We **stop tolerating mistreatment** because we **trust that Jesus is enough**.

"You teach people how to treat you by what you allow."

If you have been **allowing people to mistreat you**, it's time to stop.

No more allowing "jokes" at your expense.

No more tolerating emotional or physical abuse.

No more sacrificing yourself for people who don't value you.

It is time to **love yourself the way Jesus loves you**.

*****

Isaiah 61: God's Promise to Reverse the Pain

One night at work, I saw my phone's screensaver.

It was a picture of someone I love—**someone no longer in my life**.

And I broke down.

I had to leave the floor and take a break.

In the break room, there was a **Bible**.

I picked it up and **flipped it open randomly**.

It landed on **Isaiah 61**.

And this is what I read:

> *"The Spirit of the Sovereign LORD is on me, because the LORD has anointed me to proclaim good news to the poor. He has sent me to bind up the broken-hearted, to proclaim freedom for the captives and release from darkness for the prisoners, to proclaim*

the year of the LORD's favor and the day of vengeance of our God, to comfort all who mourn."

(Isaiah 61:1-2, NIV)

This passage describes **a new creation filled with joy and abundance**.

But before that can happen, **God must first reverse everything that's wrong.**

He was telling me:

"I am working on your situation. But it will take time."

And **that gave me hope.**

***

Don't Give Up—Your Breakthrough is Coming

If you are **walking through betrayal**, I need you to hear me:

Do not give up.

If you give up now, **you won't get to see what God is going to do next**.

> **"And we know that in all things God works for the good of those who love Him, who have been called according to His purpose."**

(Romans 8:28, NIV)

Nothing bad **lasts forever**.

The sun will rise again.

And you need to **stick around to see it.**

This will probably be **the hardest part of your journey**.

But **you will get through it**.

Because **Jesus is with you**.

And He is **with your Judas too.**

**So keep praying.
Keep trusting.
Keep believing.**

And remember—**Your Judas needs your prayers now more than ever.**

Because **only Jesus can turn their heart around.**

And **only Jesus can heal yours.**

Chapter 10

Are You in Bondage? In Jail?

A long time ago, I had a **dream**.

I was sitting in a **jail cell** when suddenly, the doors **swung open**.

Everyone else **got up and left**—but **I stayed.**

I didn't understand why.

Something **inside me felt afraid** to leave. I thought I was **doing the right thing** by staying put.

At the time, I had **no idea what that dream meant**.

But years later, I realized:

I had been keeping myself in bondage.

Not in a **physical** jail.

But in a **mental, emotional, and spiritual** one.

I had been **chaining myself** to unhealthy relationships, toxic cycles, and deep-rooted pain—choosing to **stay imprisoned** instead of walking **in the freedom God had already given me**.

***

Are You Holding Yourself Captive?

Sometimes, we stay in **unhealthy situations** because we believe **the other person needs us**.

We convince ourselves that:

- **They won't survive without us.**
- **We can "fix" them if we just love them enough.**
- **If we keep sacrificing ourselves, they'll eventually change.**

But none of this is **true**.

And in the process, we become **our own captors—** locking ourselves in prisons **we were never meant to stay in.**

***

When Love Becomes Self-Sabotage

Love should **never** require:

- **Sacrificing your well-being.**
- **Enduring constant mistreatment.**
- **Allowing someone to disrespect you repeatedly.**

That is **not love**.

That is **bondage**.

We think we're **helping them** by staying, but what we're actually doing is:

- **Teaching them that mistreating us is okay.**
- **Showing them that we don't love ourselves enough to walk away.**
- **Enabling their bad behavior instead of holding them accountable.**

***

When God Takes Away Your Peace

Sometimes, **God will allow someone to keep hurting you**—not because He wants you to suffer, but because **He wants you to leave**.

He has already **shown you the warning signs**, but if you keep ignoring them, He may allow things to escalate until you **have no choice but to go.**

Why?

Because **He loves you too much** to let you stay in a situation that is **destroying you**.

So He removes your **peace**.

He makes it **so uncomfortable** that you have **no choice** but to walk away.

And when you finally leave, you'll realize **the peace of God is better than any toxic love you left behind.**

***

God Calls You to Isolation for Healing

If you've walked away from a **toxic situation**, and now you feel alone—**it is not a punishment.**

It is an **invitation**.

God is **calling you to Himself** so that He can:

- **Heal your wounds.**
- **Break your chains.**
- **Restore what was lost.**

This is known as **the molding process**.

And yes, **it is painful**.

But **it is necessary**.

Because when God is finished with you, **you will never tolerate mistreatment again**.

You will know:

> **"The Lord is close to the brokenhearted and saves those who are crushed in spirit."**
>
> *(Psalm 34:18, NIV)*

***

You Are Not a Living Sacrifice for Others

Let me be clear:

You were **not created** to be a **living sacrifice** for other people.

Not even for the ones **you love most**.

Yes, we are called to **love and serve others**, but **not at the cost of our own destruction**.

Only Jesus was qualified to be a living sacrifice.

He took our punishment.
He endured the suffering.
He died so that **we wouldn't have to go to hell.**

You are **not their savior**.

You cannot **fix** them.

But **Jesus can**.

And that's why **letting go is sometimes the most loving thing you can do.**

***

Hearing God's Voice Through His Word

If you are struggling to hear **God's voice**, start with His **Word**.

Even if you don't understand it, **read it anyway**.

If you don't know where to begin, **ask Him**.

Pray, *"Lord, show me what You want me to know today."*

Then **flip open your Bible** and read what your eyes land on.

You may be **surprised** at how God speaks to you.

> **"Your word is a lamp to my feet and a light to my path."**
>
> *(Psalm 119:105, NIV)*

*** *

God Will Make You Stronger

This **season of isolation** is not meant to break you.

It is meant to **remake you**.

God is taking:

- **All the broken places** in your heart.
- **All the wounds from your past.**
- **All the pain you thought you'd never survive.**

And He is **mending them**.

He is making you **whole again**.

"We are all broken. That's how the light gets in."

***

The Vase Analogy

Have you ever **broken something valuable** and tried to glue it back together?

At first, you can **see the cracks**.

The pieces don't fit perfectly.

But when **light shines through it**, something **beautiful happens**—it **glows in ways it never did before**.

That's what God is doing **with you**.

He is taking what was **shattered** and turning it into **something even more beautiful.**

> **"The Lord will fight for you; you need only to be still."**
>
> *(Exodus 14:14, NIV)*

***

You Won't Let Just Anyone into Your Life Anymore

Once you have experienced **God's healing and peace**, you will **never settle for less again**.

- If someone tries to **bring toxicity into your life**, you will **send them away with love.**
- If someone refuses to **heal and grow**, you will **not carry their weight.**
- If someone does not align with **God's peace**, you will **choose to protect your own.**

Because you will **remember the pain**.

You will remember **how hard it was to heal**.

And you will refuse to **go back to where God saved you from**.

You will finally **value yourself the way Jesus values you**.

***

Jesus Is Your Safe Place

The greatest thing I've learned?

Jesus is my safe place.

He is:

- **My Best Friend.**
- **My Comforter.**
- **My Protector.**

And I never have to **beg for His love**.

I never have to **fear His rejection**.

I never have to **earn His approval**.

Because **He already loves me completely.**

And **He loves you completely too.**

So if you are still **sitting in that jail cell**, afraid to leave...

Walk out.

The doors are **already open**.

And Jesus is **waiting on the other side.**

Chapter 11

Breakups

We've all been there.

Or at least, **most of us have**.

Heartbreak.

The kind that makes it hard to breathe.

The kind that **shakes you to your core**.

It always starts the same way—**exciting, hopeful, full of promise**.

You think, *"This is the one."*

You never imagine it will end—until it **does**.

And when it does, it feels like a **death**.

Because in a way, **it is**.

The relationship **died**, and now you're left trying to figure out **how to go on without them**.

But **you will** go on.

And if you let yourself **heal properly**, you will come out of this **stronger, wiser, and better prepared for what's next**.

***

Step 1: Accept It for What It Is

The hardest part of a breakup is **accepting that it's over**.

You may replay the good times, **forgetting the bad**—but don't.

There's a **reason it ended**.

Don't **romanticize the past** so much that you lose sight of **why you walked away**.

And if they left you?

Then remember:

- **The right person would never leave.**
- **You should never have to beg for love.**
- **Love should feel safe, not uncertain.**

You have to **want** to get over it in order to **move on**.

If you don't **work on healing**, you'll rush into another relationship just to **numb the pain**.

And if you do that, you won't just be **hurting yourself—** you'll be dragging your **unhealed wounds** into something new.

***

Step 2: Pain Is Not Your Enemy—Avoiding It Is

Pain **hurts**, but it is **not your enemy**.

Pain can be your **teacher**.

- It reminds you **what not to do**.
- It helps you recognize **red flags faster**.

- It warns you **not to touch the fire again**.

You wouldn't **keep putting your hand on a hot stove**, would you?

Then don't **keep going back to what burned you in the first place**.

Let **the pain shape you**, not destroy you.

***

Step 3: Give Yourself Time to Heal

Healing isn't **pretty**.

It's crying in the middle of the night.
It's staring at your phone, resisting the urge to text them.
It's replaying conversations, wondering *"what if?"*

But **this is part of the process**.

So **allow yourself time** to:

- Cry.
- Eat junk food.
- Watch Netflix.
- Go out with friends.

- Read your Bible.

Just **don't do anything self-destructive**.

You have to go through it to get through it.

And **I promise**—this pain **won't last forever**.

***

Step 4: Own Your Part

This is the part people **don't want to hear**—but it's necessary.

What role did **you** play in the breakup?

- Did you **ignore the red flags**?
- Did you **stay too long** when the signs were clear?
- Did you **lose yourself in the relationship**?

This isn't **victim-blaming**.

It's **self-reflection**.

Because if you don't **learn from this**, you're going to **repeat it.**

Look at how you **handled conflicts**:

- Did you lash out in **anger**?
- Did you **communicate your needs** or suppress them?
- Were you **emotionally healthy** in the relationship?

Healing isn't just **moving on from them**—it's **growing into a better version of yourself**.

***

Step 5: No Contact—Seriously

Don't call.

Don't text.

Don't stalk their social media.

Don't drive by their house.

Nothing.

This is **your time to heal**.

Every time you **break no contact**, you're **ripping off the bandage** before the wound can heal.

And **every time you let them back in too soon**, you're inviting in **more pain**.

It took me **a full year of no contact** to heal from a **seven-year relationship**.

And it was the best decision I ever made.

If they **wanted to see you, they would**.

Don't **chase** someone who broke you.

***

Step 6: Make a Pros & Cons List

Write down:

- **All the reasons you left.**
- **All the times they hurt you.**
- **All the ways they let you down.**

This isn't about **staying angry**—it's about **remembering the truth**.

Because heartbreak has a way of **making us forget.**

Pray and ask **God to heal your heart** and to break **any unhealthy bonds** you feel with them.

Read **scriptures on heartbreak.**

God's love will **get you through this.**

> *"The Lord is near to the brokenhearted and saves the crushed in spirit."*
>
> *(Psalm 34:18, ESV)*

***

Step 7: Go to God First—Not Friends

Yes, **seek wise counsel.**

But **not everyone who gives advice is your friend.**

Some people just **want details.**
Some people **want to see you suffer.**
Some people **will steer you wrong on purpose.**

So before you **vent to a friend**, talk to **God first.**

Cry out to Him.
Tell Him **everything you feel**.
Then **open your Bible** and let Him **speak back to you**.

Highlight the verses **that speak to your heart**.

That is **God talking directly to you**.

The more you **read His Word**, the more **you will recognize His voice**.

And His voice will **never lead you wrong**.

***

Step 8: Forgive Yourself

This might be **the hardest part**.

- Forgive yourself for **not knowing what you didn't know**.
- Forgive yourself for **staying too long**.
- Forgive yourself for **loving the wrong person**.

It's okay.

You **won't make the same mistakes again**.

Because now, **you know better**.

***

Step 9: Don't Give Up on Life

I need you to hear me:

Do not give up.

Your **life is not over** because this relationship ended.

Nothing bad lasts forever.

The **sun will rise again**.

But if you give up now, **you'll never get to see it**.

> *"And we know that in all things God works for the good of those who love Him, who have been called according to His purpose."*
>
> *(Romans 8:28, NIV)*

***

Step 10: Use Your Pain for a Purpose

One day, **someone else will go through what you just did**.

And they'll feel **lost, broken, hopeless**.

They will need someone to:

- **Sit with them in the dark.**
- **Pray for them when they can't pray for themselves.**
- **Remind them that they will get through this.**

You will be that person.

You will take **what was meant to break you** and turn it into a **blessing for someone else**.

That is how **God redeems pain**.

***

Step 11: Know What Love Really Is

1 Corinthians 13:4-8.

4 Love is patient, love is kind. It does not envy, it does not boast, it is not proud. 5 It does not dishonor others,

it is not self-seeking, it is not easily angered, it keeps no record of wrongs. 6 Love does not delight in evil but rejoices with the truth. 7 It always protects, always trusts, always hopes, always perseveres.

8 Love never fails. But where there are prophecies, they will cease; where there are tongues, they will be stilled; where there is knowledge, it will pass away.

Does that sound like the love you had?

Be honest.

Because **real love** should look **like that.**

And if it didn't—**it wasn't love.**

Don't be afraid to be single.

Because with **Jesus, you are never alone.**

And **His love will never break your heart.**

Chapter 12

Parents, Children, and Relationships

The Hard Truth About Parenting and Relationships

A child in a home with one loving parent is far better than a child in a home with even one abusive parent.

Yet, so many of us **cling to toxic relationships**—for the sake of our children, out of fear of being alone, or simply because we don't see a way out.

We tell ourselves:

- *"They need both parents."*
- *"Maybe things will get better."*
- *"I can endure it for their sake."*

But we **fail to realize** that if someone is abusive to us, **sooner or later, they will turn that abuse toward our children too.**

And if the **abuse isn't physical**, then it may be **emotional, mental, or verbal**, which can be **just as damaging** in the long run.

***

Rushing Into the Wrong Relationships

Sometimes, after leaving an unhealthy relationship, we rush into another one—thinking:

- *"I need a father/mother figure for my kids."*
- *"They need stability."*
- *"I don't want to raise them alone."*

But **how many times have we seen these rushed relationships end in tragedy?**

The **wrong** person in a child's life is far more dangerous than **no person at all.**

We have to **be careful who we allow into our homes and around our children.**

***

God as the Father to the Fatherless

If your child is growing up without a mother or father, **remind them that they are never truly alone.**

God is their Father.

> *"Father of the fatherless and protector of widows is God in his holy habitation."*
>
> *(Psalm 68:5, ESV)*

Teach them to **turn to Jesus,** so they don't turn to the world for love, approval, and answers.

***

Breaking the Cycle of Abandonment

I know this pain firsthand.

My biological father left when I was a baby.

A year later, he came back, saying he wanted to be in my life—but my mother told him:

> *"If we can't be a family, then no—you can't be in her life at all."*

So, he left again.

That was **the first man to walk out of my life**, and it left a deep scar.

He told a relative that if I ever wanted to meet him when I was older, he would be open to it.

But by then, I thought: *"I've already grown up without him. I don't need him anymore."*

I told myself I was **okay**—but the truth is, that wound **followed me into relationships**.

I held on to **the wrong people** for far too long.

I settled for less than I deserved.

I accepted behaviors I never should have tolerated.

Because deep down, I feared **abandonment.**

***

Protecting Our Children—Even When We Don't See the Danger

It's **our job as parents** to protect our children—not just from **physical** harm, but also from emotional, mental, and spiritual harm.

That means:

- **Paying attention to how they act around certain people.**
- **Asking the hard questions—even if the answers are painful.**
- **Not blindly trusting people just because they are family or close friends.**

Even **animals can sense danger** before we do.

If **your pet is acting off around someone**, take that as a **red flag**.

And most importantly, **if your child is uncomfortable around someone, believe them.**

***

Knowing What You Don't Know

No matter how much we **watch over them**, sometimes **bad things still happen.**

We **can't know what they don't tell us.**

And some kids **won't talk—**

- Because they don't feel safe.
- Because they don't know how to put it into words.
- Because they fear they won't be believed.

Even if you've asked the right questions...
Even if you've done **everything** to protect them...
Even if you **love them unconditionally**...

Some wounds stay buried until years later.

And one day, when those wounds resurface, they may **blame you.**

They may **lash out in anger, resentment, and pain.**

They may **walk out of your life completely.**

***

When Your Children Turn Against You

Nothing prepares you for **the pain of your child blaming you for something you didn't even know happened.**

It will feel like **a betrayal, a punishment, an unbearable weight.**

But **don't react in anger**.

Don't get **defensive**.

Listen.

- Even if it's hard to hear.
- Even if they are wrong about some things.
- Even if their anger is misplaced.

You may not **agree with everything they say**—but acknowledge their **pain**.

Even if you **didn't mean to cause harm**, harm still happened.

And **they need to heal.**

If they decide to **cut you out of their life, let them go—** but never stop **praying for them.**

***

The Spiritual Battle for Your Children

This is where **your fight changes.**

Your battle is **no longer physical—**it is **spiritual.**

The enemy wants to **steal them away.**

He wants you to **give up on them.**

But you **CANNOT.**

Even if they reject you.
Even if they don't believe in God right now.
Even if they don't speak to you anymore.

Pray for them anyway.

Fast for them.

Stand in the gap for them.

"A voice is heard in Ramah, weeping and great mourning, Rachel weeping for her children and refusing to be comforted, because they are no more."

This is what the Lord says: 'Restrain your voice from weeping and your eyes from tears, for your work will be rewarded,' declares the Lord. 'They will return from the land of the enemy. So there is hope for your descendants,' declares the Lord. 'Your children will return to their own land.'"

(Jeremiah 31:15-17, ESV)

***

Hold On—Even When It Hurts

If you've lost your family...
If you've lost **everyone** you love...
If you feel like you **have no reason left to live**...

This is why you must stay.

Because **your children still need you to pray for them**.

If you don't pray for them, **who will?**

If you give up now, **who will fight for them?**

***

The Devil is After Our Children

Why do you think Satan **goes after children so hard?**

Because if he can **break them before they find Jesus,** he can **keep them from fulfilling their God-given purpose.**

Jesus Himself warned us:

> *"It would be better for them to be thrown into the sea with a millstone tied around their neck than to cause one of these little ones to stumble."*
>
> *(Luke 17:2, NIV)*

Satan doesn't just **hate us**—he hates **God.**

And what better way to **hurt God** than to **steal His children away?**

***

God's Got You

For those of you struggling with **forgiving your parents,** please remember:

It took those two people to create you.

Nobody else could have brought **you** into this world.

You **had to be here**—because God has **a purpose for your life**.

Even if your parents failed you...
Even if they weren't what you needed them to be...

God **never fails.**

And **He can heal every wound—yours, your parents', and your children's.**

Trust Him.

And keep fighting.

You've got this—because of the One who's got you.

Chapter 13

Barabbas—A Picture of Redemption

Have you ever heard the story of **Barabbas**?

He was **a murderer**, **a criminal**, and **a rebel against authority**. A **notorious prisoner**, hated by many but also followed by those who rejected Roman rule.

He was imprisoned at the same time as **Jesus**—and on the day of Jesus' trial, **his life was in the hands of the people**.

***

The Choice Between Jesus and Barabbas

Pilate, the Roman governor, stood before a restless crowd.

It was **tradition** during the Passover feast for the governor to **release one prisoner** to the people.

That day, he gave them a choice:

- **Jesus of Nazareth**—the innocent, loving, miracle-working Son of God, who healed the sick, raised the dead, and cast out demons.
- **Barabbas**—a **violent murderer**, a **thief**, and a **rebel** against the government.

Who did the crowd choose?

Barabbas.

They demanded **freedom for the murderer** and **death for the Savior.**

> *"Which of the two do you want me to release to you?" asked the governor.*
> *"Barabbas," they answered.*
> *"What shall I do, then, with Jesus who is called the Messiah?" Pilate asked.*
> *They all answered, "Crucify him!"*
>
> *(Matthew 27:15-26, NIV)*

Jesus stood **silently** as they condemned Him.

He did **not** fight back.
He did **not** plead for mercy.
He did **not** try to defend Himself.

Instead, **He took Barabbas' place**—and not just his place, but **ours too.**

***

Jesus Took Barabbas' Punishment—and Ours

Barabbas walked free that day, but not because he was innocent.

He was guilty of **insurrection, murder, and rebellion**—crimes punishable by death.

But **Jesus took his punishment**.

Do you see the symbolism here?

We are Barabbas.

Just like him, we have sinned.

Just like him, we were **condemned**—but Jesus **took our place** so we could go free.

Romans 5:8 says:

> *"But God demonstrates His own love for us in this: While we were still sinners, Christ died for us."*

He didn't wait for us to **get our lives together**.

He didn't say, **"Clean yourself up first, then I'll help you."**

While we were **still sinners**, still making mistakes, still lost in our old ways, **He chose to suffer and die for us.**

That is **grace**.

That is **love**.

***

The Crowd Chose a Murderer Over a Savior

It's easy to wonder, *"How could they choose Barabbas over Jesus?"*

But look at today's world.

People still reject Jesus.

They **choose sin** over salvation.
They **choose temporary pleasure** over eternal life.
They **choose rebellion** over repentance.

The crowd **mocked** Jesus, spat on Him, and called for His **crucifixion**—even after He healed their sick, cast out their demons, and fed them when they were hungry.

And still, **He loved them.**

He didn't just die for the **righteous**—He died for the **murderers, the thieves, the liars, the addicts, and the broken.**

***

No Sin is Greater Than His Mercy

People often wonder:

> *"Will God really forgive me?"*
> *"How can He love me after all I've done?"*
> *"What if I've messed up too many times?"*

Let me tell you something—**no sin is too great for His mercy.**

You can be forgiven.

No matter your past.
No matter your failures.
No matter how many times you've fallen.

> *"If we confess our sins, He is faithful and just to forgive us our sins and to cleanse us from all unrighteousness."*
>
> *(1 John 1:9, ESV)*

You may feel like **you don't deserve forgiveness**—but **none of us do.**

That's the beauty of grace.

Barabbas didn't deserve to walk free.

But Jesus took his place anyway.

You and I don't deserve **mercy, love, or salvation**.

But Jesus took our place anyway.

That's **who He is.**

***

What Will You Choose?

Barabbas thought **the people set him free**—but it was **Jesus who took his punishment**.

The real question is:

Now that Jesus has taken **your punishment**, what will you do with that freedom?

Will you go back to your old ways?
Will you ignore the sacrifice He made for you?
Or will you surrender your life to the One who gave His life for you?

Jesus is standing before you today, offering you **forgiveness, freedom, and eternal life**.

Will you **choose Him**, or will you let Him walk away like the crowd did that day?

***

It's Not Too Late to Come Home

If you've been running from Jesus, **it's not too late to turn back.**

He's **not angry with you.**

He's **not waiting to punish you.**

He's standing with **open arms**, ready to forgive, to heal, and to restore you.

All you have to do is **come home.**

> *"Come to me, all who are weary and burdened, and I will give you rest."*
>
> *(Matthew 11:28, NIV)*

***

Jesus is Enough

No matter what you've done.
No matter how many times you've failed.
No matter how far you've strayed.

Jesus **is enough.**

He is **strong enough to carry your burdens.**
He is **merciful enough to forgive your sins.**
He is **loving enough to walk with you every step of the way.**

You don't have to **fight this battle alone**.

You don't have to **try to be perfect**.

Just **come to Him** as you are—and let **His grace do the rest.**

***

The Choice is Yours

Today, you stand where **Barabbas stood.**

Jesus **already paid the price** for your freedom.

The question is—**what will you do with it?**

Will you continue down the **same path**?

Or will you **turn to Him** and receive the greatest gift of all—**a new life in Christ**?

The choice is yours.

But whatever you decide—**know that Jesus is waiting for you.**

And **His love has never left you.**

- **He took your place.**
- **He set you free.**
- **Now, walk in that freedom.**

Chapter 14

Know Your Identity in Christ

There is a reason the devil is working so hard to make you **forget who you are** and **whose you are**.

He wants to confuse you.

He wants to distract you.

He wants to steal your purpose, your confidence, and your identity in **Jesus Christ** before you can fully realize the power of who God created you to be.

Satan has been attacking **identity** since the beginning of time. He did it with **Eve in the Garden**, he did it with **Jesus in the wilderness**, and he is doing it now in the hearts of **God's children**—especially **the young and vulnerable**.

- He creates **confusion**—about gender, purpose, relationships, and self-worth.
- He plants **doubt**—"Did God really say that?" (Genesis 3:1).
- He fills the world with **lies**—"You are not enough," "You will never be free," "You are too broken to be loved."

But I have **good news**:

JESUS HAS ALREADY GIVEN YOU YOUR TRUE IDENTITY.

Your identity is not in your past.
Your identity is not in your trauma.
Your identity is not in your mistakes.
Your identity is **not in the lies the enemy has told you.**

Your identity is **in Christ.**

And **when you know who you are in Christ, the devil loses his power over you.**

***

Come As You Are—Let Jesus Transform You

If you feel **lost, confused, or broken**, know this:

Jesus **is not waiting for you to "fix yourself" before coming to Him.**
He is calling you **exactly as you are, right now.**
He **will help you** become who He created you to be.

Jesus **did not come to condemn** you. He came to **set you free**.

> *"For God did not send His Son into the world to condemn the world, but to save the world through Him."*
>
> *—John 3:17*

It doesn't matter how lost you feel right now.

God is calling you.

The more you spend time in His **Word**, in **prayer**, and in **His presence**, the more you will begin to **see yourself the way He sees you.**

Let's take a look at **who God says you are**.

***

Who You Are in Christ

Here are **20 powerful truths** from Scripture about your identity:

1. You Are a New Creation

"Therefore, if anyone is in Christ, the new creation has come: The old has gone, the new is here!"

(2 Corinthians 5:17)

2. You Are a Child of God

"Yet to all who did receive Him, to those who believed in His name, He gave the right to become children of God."

(John 1:12)

3. You Are a Branch of the True Vine

"I am the vine; you are the branches. If you remain in me and I in you, you will bear much fruit; apart from me you can do nothing."

(John 15:5)

4. You Are a Friend of Jesus

"I no longer call you servants, because a servant does not know his master's business. Instead, I have called you friends."

(John 15:15)

5. You Are Justified and Redeemed

"And are justified by His grace as a gift, through the redemption that is in Christ Jesus."

(Romans 3:24)

6. You Are an Heir of God

"Now if we are children, then we are heirs—heirs of God and co-heirs with Christ."

(Romans 8:17)

7. You Are Sanctified and Called to Be Holy

"To the church of God in Corinth, to those sanctified in Christ Jesus and called to be His holy people."

(1 Corinthians 1:2)

8. You Are a Temple of the Holy Spirit

"Do you not know that your bodies are temples of the Holy Spirit, who is in you, whom you have received from God? You are not your own."

(1 Corinthians 6:19)

9. You Are a Member of Christ's Body

"Now you are the body of Christ, and each one of you is a part of it."

(1 Corinthians 12:27)

10. You Are an Ambassador for Christ

"We are therefore Christ's ambassadors, as though God were making His appeal through us."

(2 Corinthians 5:20)

11. You Are the Righteousness of God

"God made Him who had no sin to be sin for us, so that in Him we might become the righteousness of God."

(2 Corinthians 5:21)

12. You Are Chosen

"For He chose us in Him before the creation of the world to be holy and blameless in His sight."

(Ephesians 1:4)

13. You Are Adopted into God's Family

"He predestined us for adoption to sonship through Jesus Christ, in accordance with His pleasure and will."

(Ephesians 1:5)

14. You Are Redeemed and Forgiven

"In Him we have redemption through His blood, the forgiveness of sins, in accordance with the riches of God's grace."

(Ephesians 1:7)

15. You Are Sealed with the Holy Spirit

"When you believed, you were marked in Him with a seal, the promised Holy Spirit."

(Ephesians 1:13)

16. You Are Made Alive in Christ

"But because of His great love for us, God, who is rich in mercy, made us alive with Christ."

(Ephesians 2:4-5)

17. You Are Raised and Seated with Christ

"And God raised us up with Christ and seated us with Him in the heavenly realms in Christ Jesus."

(Ephesians 2:6)

18. You Are God's Masterpiece

"For we are God's handiwork, created in Christ Jesus to do good works, which God prepared in advance for us to do."

(Ephesians 2:10)

19. You Are a Citizen of Heaven

"But our citizenship is in heaven. And we eagerly await a Savior from there, the Lord Jesus Christ."

(Philippians 3:20)

20. You Are Free in Christ

"It is for freedom that Christ has set us free. Stand firm, then, and do not let yourselves be burdened again by a yoke of slavery."

(Galatians 5:1)

***

Walk in Your True Identity

When you **know your identity in Christ**, the lies of the enemy lose power over you.

You are **not** your past.
You are **not** your mistakes.
You are **not** what others have said about you.

You are chosen.
You are loved.
You are redeemed.

You are a child of God.

Now that you know **who you are**, will you start walking in the **freedom, confidence, and purpose** that God has given you?

Don't let the devil steal **your identity**.

Stand firm.
Walk boldly.
Live as **who God created you to be.**

Because **you belong to Jesus**—and that is more than enough.

Chapter 15

Backing Up What You Say with Scriptures

If you're anything like me, **you hate confrontation and conflict.**

You don't want to offend anyone, and yet, in today's world, it seems **almost impossible** not to.

People get defensive when you bring up God's truth. They get angry when you talk about **right and wrong**. They accuse you of **judging** them when you try to help.

And yet, as **followers of Christ**, we are **called to stand for truth**—not in a harsh or condemning way, but **in love, with grace and wisdom.**

"Let your conversation be always full of grace, seasoned with salt, so that you may know how to answer everyone."

—Colossians 4:6

***

The Difference Between Judging and Holding Someone Accountable

One of the biggest **misconceptions** people have today is what it means to **judge** someone versus **holding them accountable in love**.

Judging is looking down on someone with **pride and self-righteousness**, thinking you are better than they are.
Judging is pointing fingers **without offering solutions, guidance, or grace**.
Judging is gossiping, condemning, and mocking others for their sins **while ignoring your own**.

But that is **NOT** what Jesus calls us to do.

Holding someone accountable is lovingly pointing them back to God's truth.
Holding someone accountable is **not** about personal opinions, but about **what God's Word says**.

Holding someone accountable is done **out of love, not pride or condemnation**.

> *"Brothers and sisters, if someone is caught in a sin, you who live by the Spirit should restore that person gently. But watch yourselves, or you also may be tempted."*
>
> *—Galatians 6:1*

When you lovingly bring **Scripture** into the conversation, it removes **you** from the equation and makes it clear that this is **God's direction, not your personal judgment.**

***

The Word of God is Our Foundation

When people say, **"Don't judge me!"** they often misunderstand what the Bible actually says about judgment.

Let's take a look at what **Scripture really teaches**:

1. The Bible Tells Us to Judge Righteously, Not Hypocritically

Many people quote **Matthew 7:1** — "Do not judge, or you too will be judged." But they forget to read the full passage.

> *"Do not judge, or you too will be judged. For in the same way you judge others, you will be judged, and with the measure you use, it will be measured to you.*
>
> *(Matthew 7:1-2)*

Jesus wasn't saying **never judge**. He was warning against **hypocritical judgment**—judging others while refusing to deal with your **own sin**.

Later in the same chapter, Jesus actually tells **believers** to be discerning:

> *"Watch out for false prophets. They come to you in sheep's clothing, but inwardly they are ferocious wolves. By their fruit, you will recognize them."*
>
> *(Matthew 7:15-16)*

This means we **must** judge **right from wrong**—but we must do it **with wisdom, humility, and love.**

2. Correcting Others Should Be Done in Love, Not Condemnation

Some people love pointing out others' faults **just to criticize**. But that's not what God calls us to do.

> *"Speak the truth in love, so that we will grow to become in every respect the mature body of Him who is the head, that is, Christ."*
>
> *(Ephesians 4:15)*

When you speak the **truth in love**, it means:

- You care about the person's **soul**, not just their behavior.
- You approach them **with humility**, knowing you are **not perfect either**.
- You **point them to Jesus**, not just tell them what they're doing wrong.

3. Sin is Serious—But God's Grace is Greater

Some people think **God doesn't care about sin** because He is "all love." But **true love warns** against destruction.

> *"For the wages of sin is death, but the gift of God is eternal life in Christ Jesus our Lord."*
>
> *(Romans 6:23)*

Jesus didn't die on the cross **so we could live however we want**. He died to **set us free from sin**, not to excuse it.

This is why the Bible calls us to **help bring others back to the truth**:

> *"My brothers and sisters, if one of you should wander from the truth and someone should bring that person back, remember this: Whoever turns a sinner from the error of their way will save them from death and cover over a multitude of sins."*

> *(James 5:19-20)*

It is **not unloving** to warn someone about sin. It is actually **one of the most loving things you can do**.

But it must always be done **with humility, kindness, and a heart that desires to help, not hurt**.

***

How to Back Up What You Say with Scripture

When you **talk to someone about sin**, always bring **God's Word** into the conversation.

Here's why:

- It takes **you** out of the equation. It's **not your opinion**, it's God's truth.
- It shows them that **this is about love and correction, not condemnation**.
- It gives them a **clear standard**—God's Word, not human ideas.

Example Conversations Backed by Scripture

Situation: Someone is living in sexual sin, but they don't think it's wrong.

Response:

> *"I know this might be hard to hear, but God calls us to live in purity. It's not about rules—it's about His best for us."*
>
> *"It is God's will that you should be sanctified: that you should avoid sexual immorality; that each of you should learn to control your own body in a way that is holy and honorable."*
>
> *(1 Thessalonians 4:3-4)*

Situation: A friend is constantly gossiping and speaking negatively about others.

Response:

"I love you, but I think we should be careful with our words. God calls us to speak life, not tear others down."

"Do not let any unwholesome talk come out of your mouths, but only what is helpful for building others up according to their needs, that it may benefit those who listen."

(Ephesians 4:29)

Situation: Someone says they love God, but they don't want to change their lifestyle.

Response:

"Loving Jesus means following Him, even when it's hard. His way is always better."

"Whoever claims to live in Him must live as Jesus did."

(1 John 2:6)

***

Speak Truth, But Speak It in Love

- **Be bold in sharing God's truth.**
- **Use Scripture to support what you say.**
- **Always speak with love, not condemnation.**

Not everyone will **listen**. Not everyone will **accept correction**. But our job is not to **convince people**—our job is to **speak truth and let God work in their hearts**.

And remember: **If you truly love someone, you won't be silent when you see them walking toward destruction.**

Stand firm. Speak truth. And always love like Jesus.

Chapter 16

Prayers for All

I believe that **our main purpose here on earth** is simple: **we are all here, trying to help each other get back Home.**

Some of us have had the hardest "teachers" out here—people who came into our lives to break us, to challenge us, to push us beyond our limits. But even in our **deepest pain**, there is a lesson. **Even in heartbreak, there is purpose.**

Those moments when I've had my heart shattered—when I've felt like I couldn't take another breath—I have run back to Jesus **like a little girl running to her Daddy**, seeking comfort, healing, and restoration. That's what He is to us—**a loving Father, a safe place, the One who makes all things new.**

But here's something important to understand:

**Those who hurt us are often hurting themselves.
The broken people who broke us need healing too.
God can even use pain to bring us closer to Him.**

That doesn't mean we excuse what people have done. It doesn't mean we allow abuse, mistreatment, or toxicity. **But it does mean that every single battle, every heartbreak, and every betrayal can point us back to Jesus.**

> *"The Lord is close to the brokenhearted and saves those who are crushed in spirit."*
>
> —*Psalm 34:18*

Even when we get lost. Even when we turn to things we shouldn't. Even when we wander away from Him—Jesus will never stop pursuing us.

The Parable of the Lost Sheep

> *"What do you think? If a man owns a hundred sheep, and one of them wanders away, will he not leave the ninety-nine on the hills and go to look for the one that wandered off? And if he finds it, truly I tell you, he is happier about that one sheep than about the*

ninety-nine that did not wander off. In the same way your Father in heaven is not willing that any of these little ones should perish."

(Matthew 18:12-14)

Jesus will leave the 99 to go after YOU.

He loves you **that much.**

***

Healing, Forgiveness, and Letting Go

In order to move forward, **we must heal.**

In order to heal, **we must forgive.**

Not for them.
Not because they deserve it.
But because YOU deserve peace.

Bitterness is a **trap from the enemy**. If you allow **anger, resentment, and unforgiveness** to settle into your heart, **it will destroy you from the inside out.**

The devil wants you to be stuck in that pain. **But Jesus wants to set you free.**

"For if you forgive other people when they sin against you, your heavenly Father will also forgive you. But if you do not forgive others their sins, your Father will not forgive your sins."

(Matthew 6:14-15)

Forgiveness **does not mean you allow people to keep hurting you.**
Forgiveness **does not mean you go back to toxic relationships.**

It means you give the pain to God.
It means you stop carrying that weight.
It means you let Jesus be the One to deal with it.

Let go.
Trust Jesus.
Keep looking up.

***

Your Soul and a Prayer for Salvation

I need you to hear me when I say this:

Your soul is NOT yours to sell.

No matter what you've done.
No matter where you've been.

No matter even if you've made **a deal with the devil himself—**
Satan is a liar, and that contract is a LIE.

Your soul has ALWAYS belonged to God.

Even if you signed a contract.
Even if you made a blood sacrifice.
Even if you did the worst things imaginable—

Jesus still forgives you.
Jesus still wants you.
Jesus still loves you.

And **right now**, He is **calling you back home.**

> *"The thief comes only to steal and kill and destroy; I have come that they may have life, and have it to the full."*
>
> *(John 10:10)*

No deal you have ever made can override **the power of the blood of Jesus Christ.**

So if you're ready to **break free**—if you're ready to **come back home**—pray this prayer with me:

***

A Prayer for Salvation

"Lord Jesus, forgive me of my sins, for all of them. Come into my heart and remember me in Your Kingdom. I believe You died for me and for my sins to save me from Hell. Thank You for Your love, for Your mercy, and for Your grace. I choose You. I accept You as my Lord and Savior. Please lead me, guide me, and help me walk in Your ways. I am Yours. In Jesus' name, Amen."

Or if you don't know what to say, **say what the thief on the cross said to Jesus:**

"Jesus, forgive me of my sins and remember me in Your Kingdom."

That's all it takes.

Because **Jesus hears you.**
Because **Jesus loves you.**
Because **Jesus already paid the price.**

"Everyone who calls on the name of the Lord will be saved."

(Romans 10:13)

***

Now What?

If you just prayed that prayer, you have **just made the most important decision of your life.**

Now, it's time to **start your journey with Jesus**:

Start reading your Bible. (If you don't know where to start, begin with the book of John.)
Talk to God every day. (Prayer isn't fancy words—it's just conversation with your Heavenly Father.)
Find a good Bible-believing church. (You need a community to help you grow.)
Turn away from the things that pull you away from God.

Jesus didn't just **die for you**—He **rose again for you.**

And that means **you have a future.**
You have **a purpose.**
You have **a new life ahead of you.**

You are forgiven.
You are free.
And you are His.

I love you.
Jesus loves you even more.

And I will be praying for you.

***

Keep Looking Up

The world is full of **pain**.
The enemy is full of **lies**.
But **Jesus is the Truth, and the Truth sets you free.**

Don't let this world steal your **joy**.
Don't let the enemy steal your **peace**.
And don't let your past define your **future**.

You are **loved.**
You are **forgiven.**
You are **a child of God.**

Keep your eyes on Jesus.
Keep your heart full of faith.
And keep going.

Because **your story isn't over.**

Continued prayers for everyone.

Chapter 17

Healing Takes Time

I truly believe that our **main purpose here on earth** is **to help each other get back Home**—to Jesus.

Some of us have had **the hardest teachers** in this life—people who broke us, betrayed us, and left scars so deep we thought we'd never heal. But even in **our deepest pain, there is a lesson**. Even in heartbreak, **there is purpose**.

When I've had my heart shattered—when I've felt like I couldn't take another breath—I have **run back to Jesus like a little girl running to her Daddy**. And every time, He has been there—ready to comfort, to heal, and to restore.

But here's something I need you to know:

**Those who hurt us are often hurting themselves.
The broken people who broke us need healing too.
God can use even pain to bring us closer to Him.**

That **doesn't mean we excuse what people have done.**
That **doesn't mean we allow mistreatment or abuse.**

But it does mean that **every battle, every heartbreak, and every betrayal can point us back to Jesus**—if we let it.

> *"The Lord is close to the brokenhearted and saves those who are crushed in spirit."*
> —*Psalm 34:18*

***

Letting Go and Trusting God

One of the hardest things to do is **letting go**—especially when it comes to our **children, our loved ones, and the people we hold dearest.**

It is vitally important that you realize something:

If you have been **owning up to your mistakes**...
If you have been **working on your healing**...
If you have **tried to make your wrongs right**...

Then **you are NOT the same person** you were in your past.

But the people who were affected—especially **our children**—are also **on their own healing journey.** And sometimes, **that means they need distance**.

You may have to let them go physically, but never spiritually.
You can still pray for them.
You can still send them love, healing, life, and light in your prayers.

Healing takes time.

Things didn't happen overnight, and most of the time, they **won't be fixed overnight** either.

But **trust God in this.**

Trust Him **to do what you cannot do**.
Trust Him **to heal what you cannot heal**.

We have to **step aside and get out of His way** so He can work.

Remember: He is the Great Physician. The **Ultimate Healer**.

Nothing is impossible for Him.
Nothing is too hard for Him.
There is **nothing He cannot fix**.

And **while God is working on your children's healing**, it is **just as important** that you **keep working on yourself**.

Keep healing.
Keep growing.
Keep becoming **the best version of yourself** that you can be.

Letting go is hard. But when you **release them from your hands into God's hands—**

There is **no greater set of hands to release them into**
There is **no love stronger than the One who loves them more than you ever could.**

And that, my friends, **is our sweet Jesus.**

I love you. I am praying for you.

I **pray that this book gives you encouragement** and that you find **peace in the broken places** in your life—**where you need love and light the most.**

***

Something to Think About on Your Healing Journey

It's been my experience—and maybe you've found this to be true as well—**that sometimes, it takes that gut-wrenching, soul-crushing pain from the people we love the most to create real change within us.**

It had to be them.
It had to be that heartbreak.
It had to be those life-altering lessons.

Because without that **devastating blow**...
Without that **moment that knocked you to your knees**...
Without that **pain that took your breath away**...

You wouldn't have grown into **who you are now**.

It had to be them, because nobody else could have gotten you there.
Nobody else could have pushed you to the place where you finally turned to Jesus.

I know—without a **shadow of a doubt**—that I **wouldn't be who I am right now** without the heartbreaks, betrayals, and losses I've endured.

SHATTERED

And I know, beyond all else, that **without Jesus, I wouldn't have survived any of it.**

So, if you are in **a season of heartbreak...**
If you feel like **you've lost everything...**
If you feel like **you don't know how to move forward...**

Remember this:

Jesus is still writing your story.
Jesus still has a plan for your life.
Jesus will use even this pain for something beautiful.

Don't give up before you see the other side.

You are **not alone**.
You are **not forgotten**.
And **you are deeply, fiercely, and unconditionally loved.**

Keep healing.
Keep trusting.
Keep looking up.

You've got this—because the One who holds the universe in His hands is holding you, too.

With love and prayers always,
Jesus loves you more than you could ever imagine.